Time to doodle to your hearts content ...

Copyright 2018 Cool Journal Creations

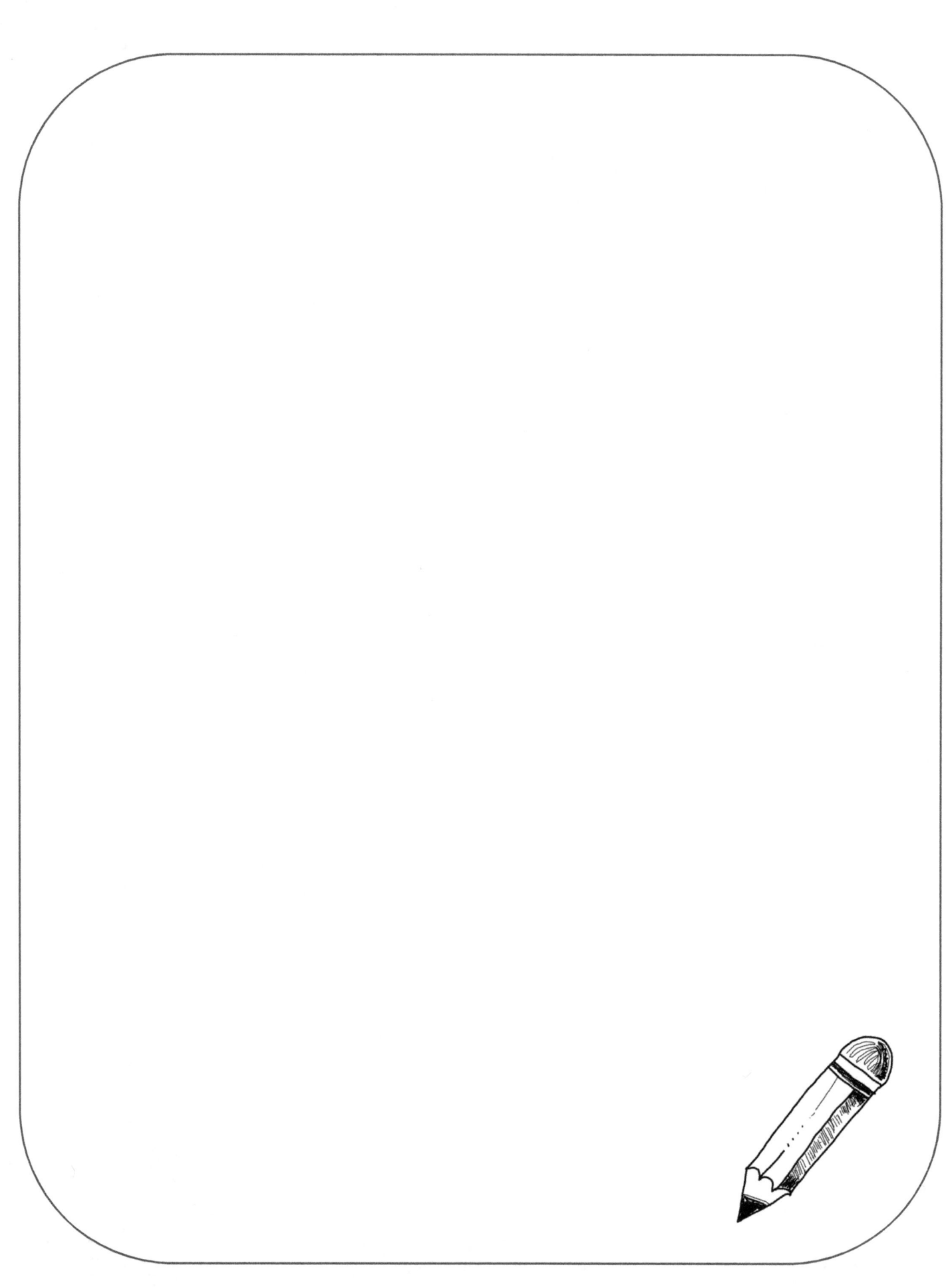

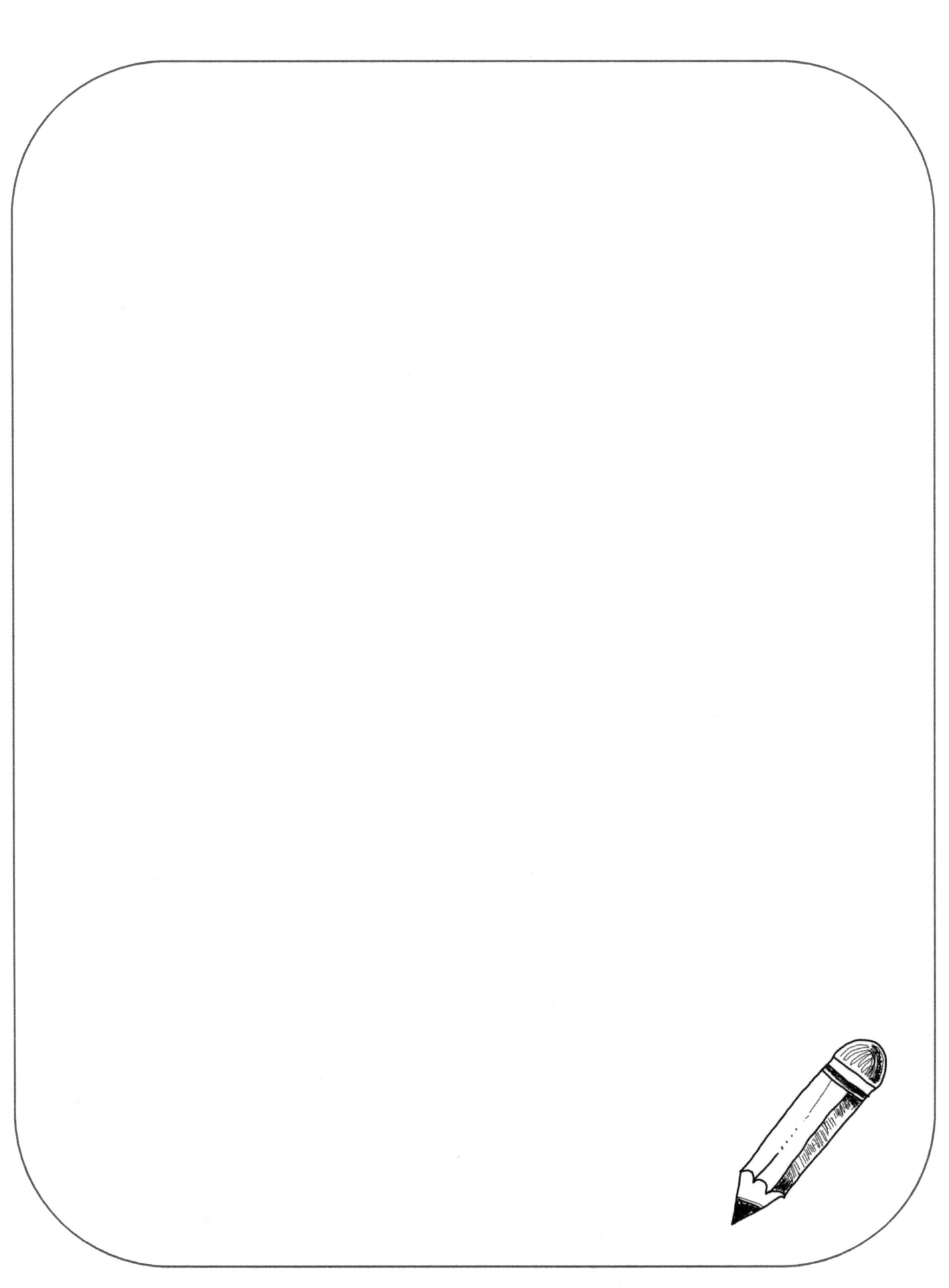

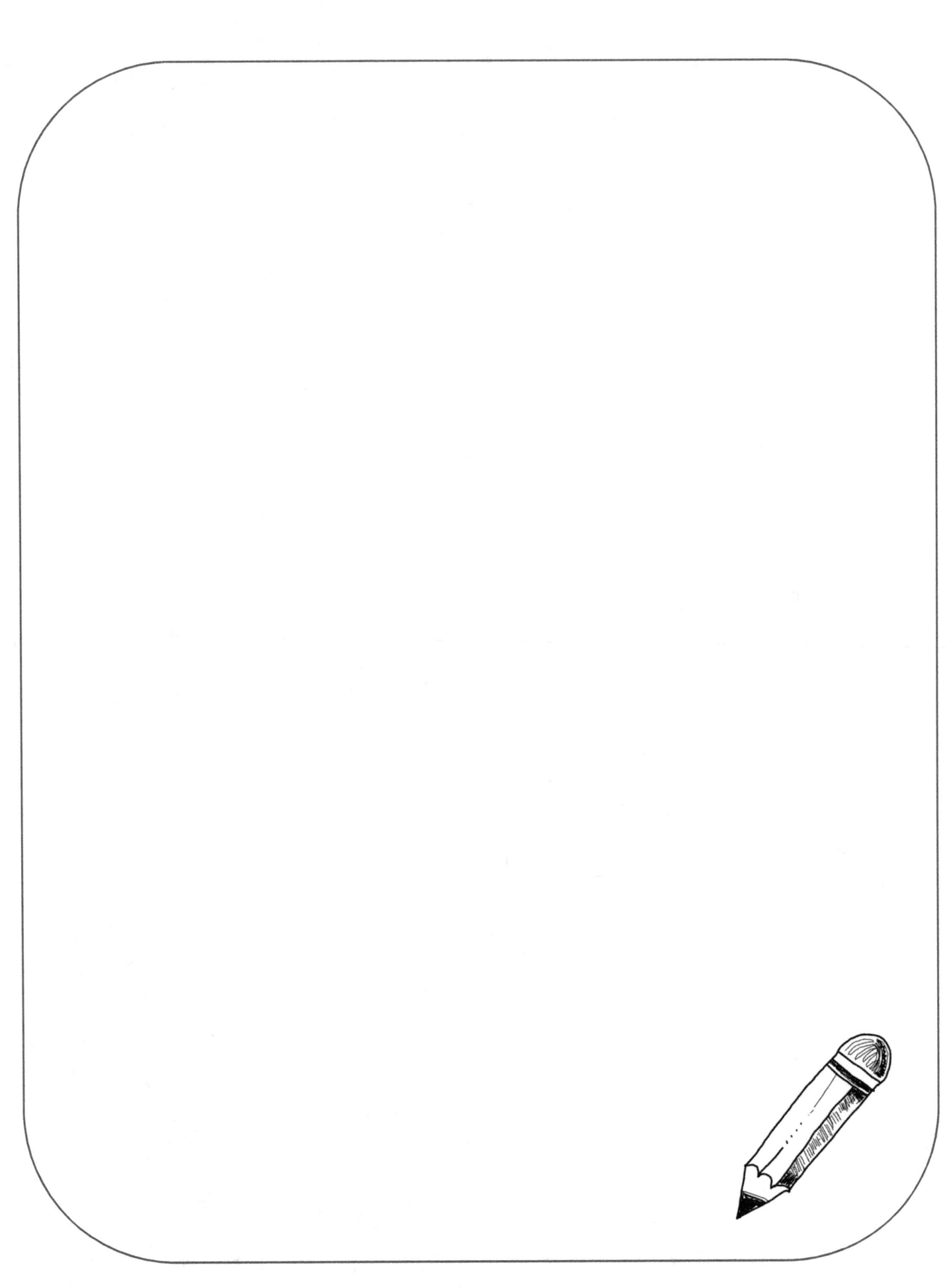

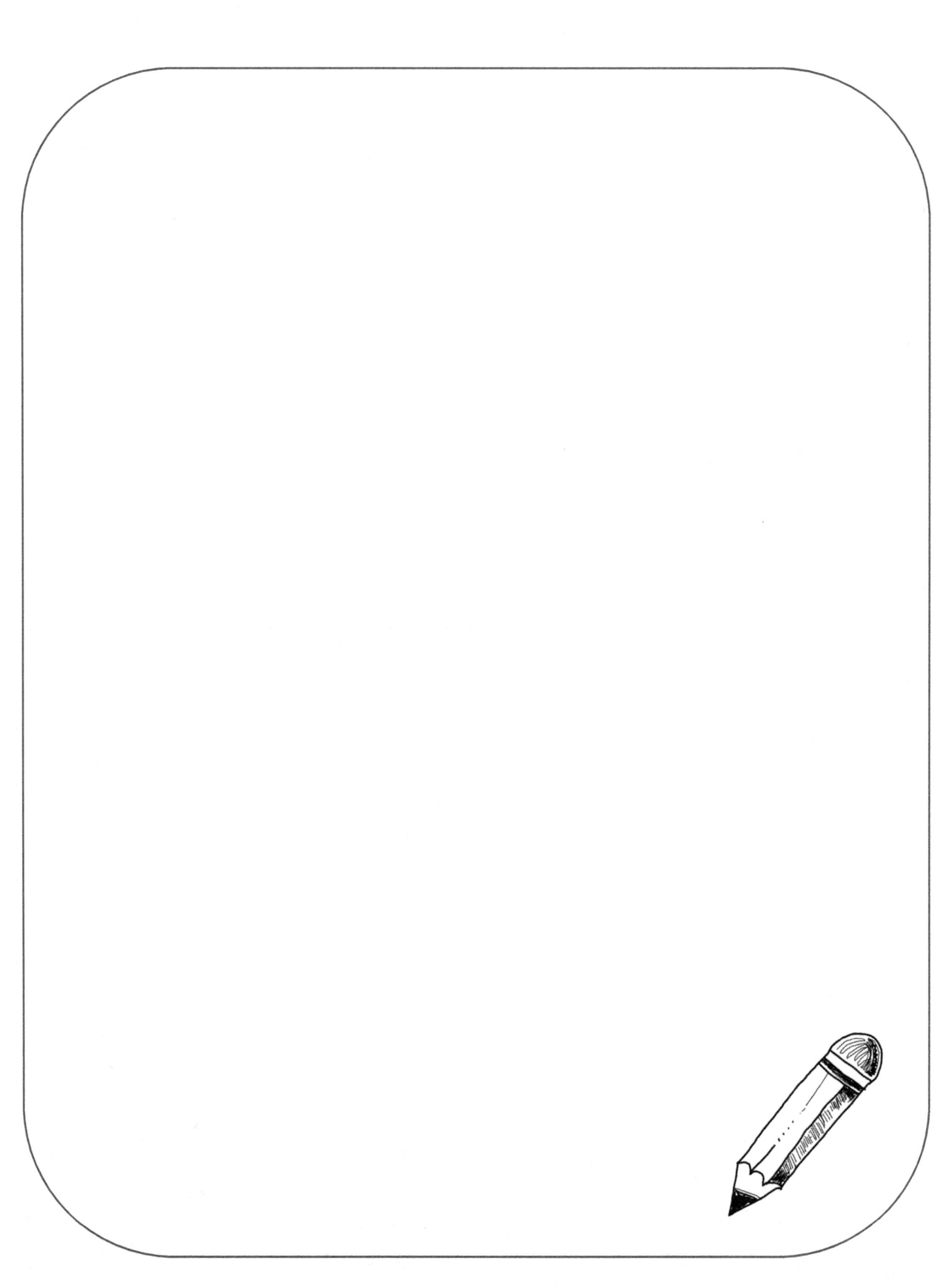

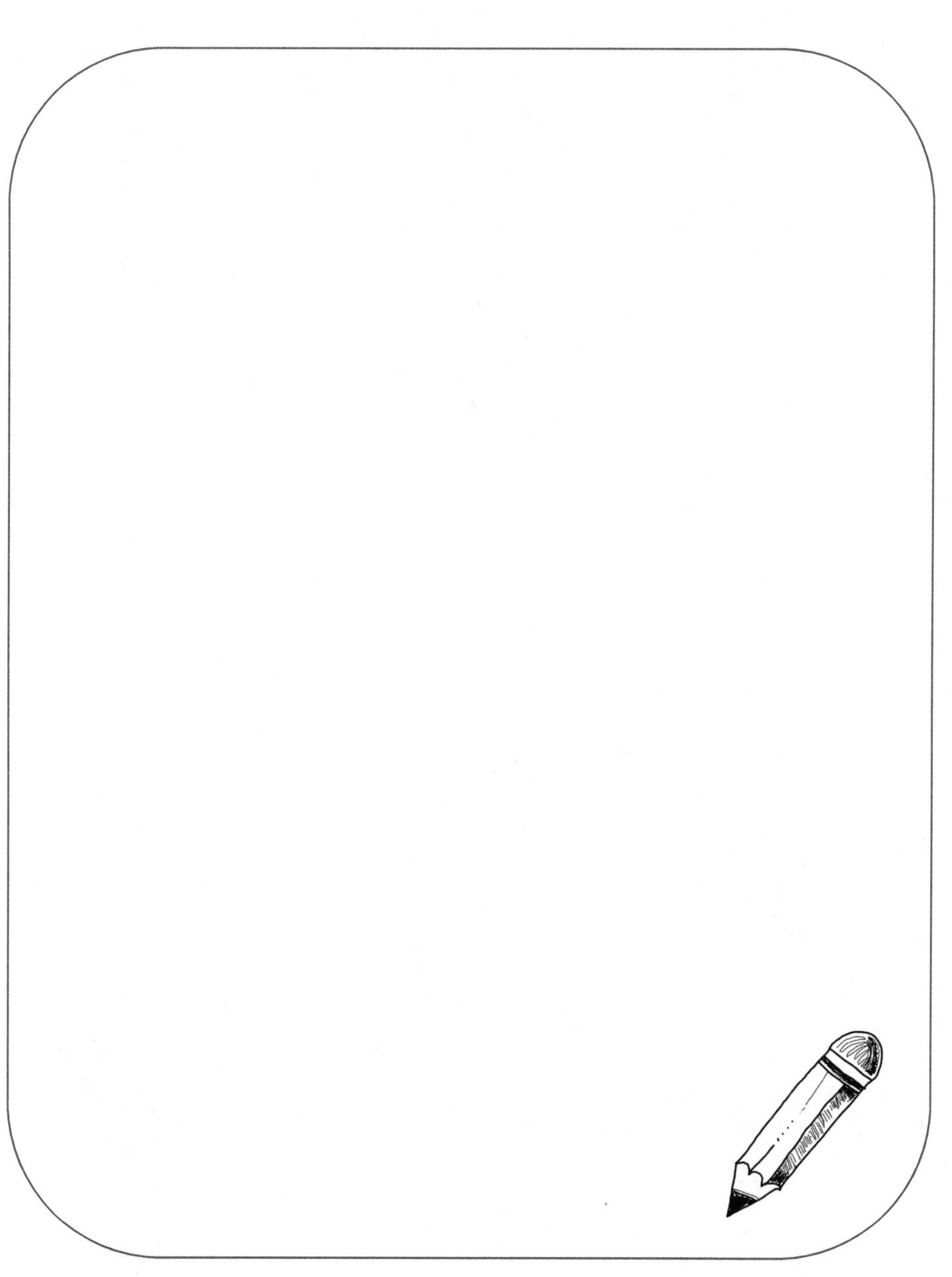

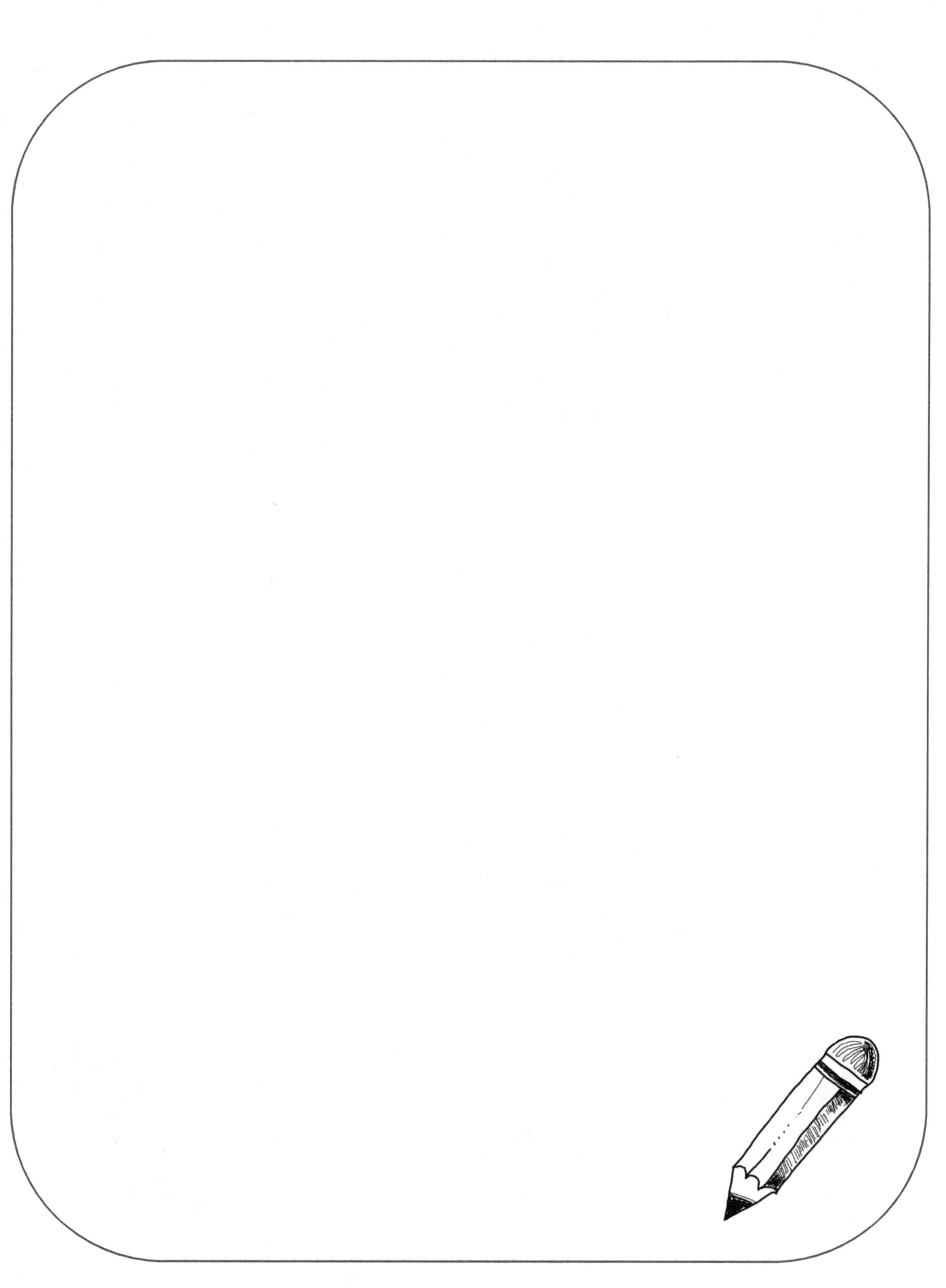

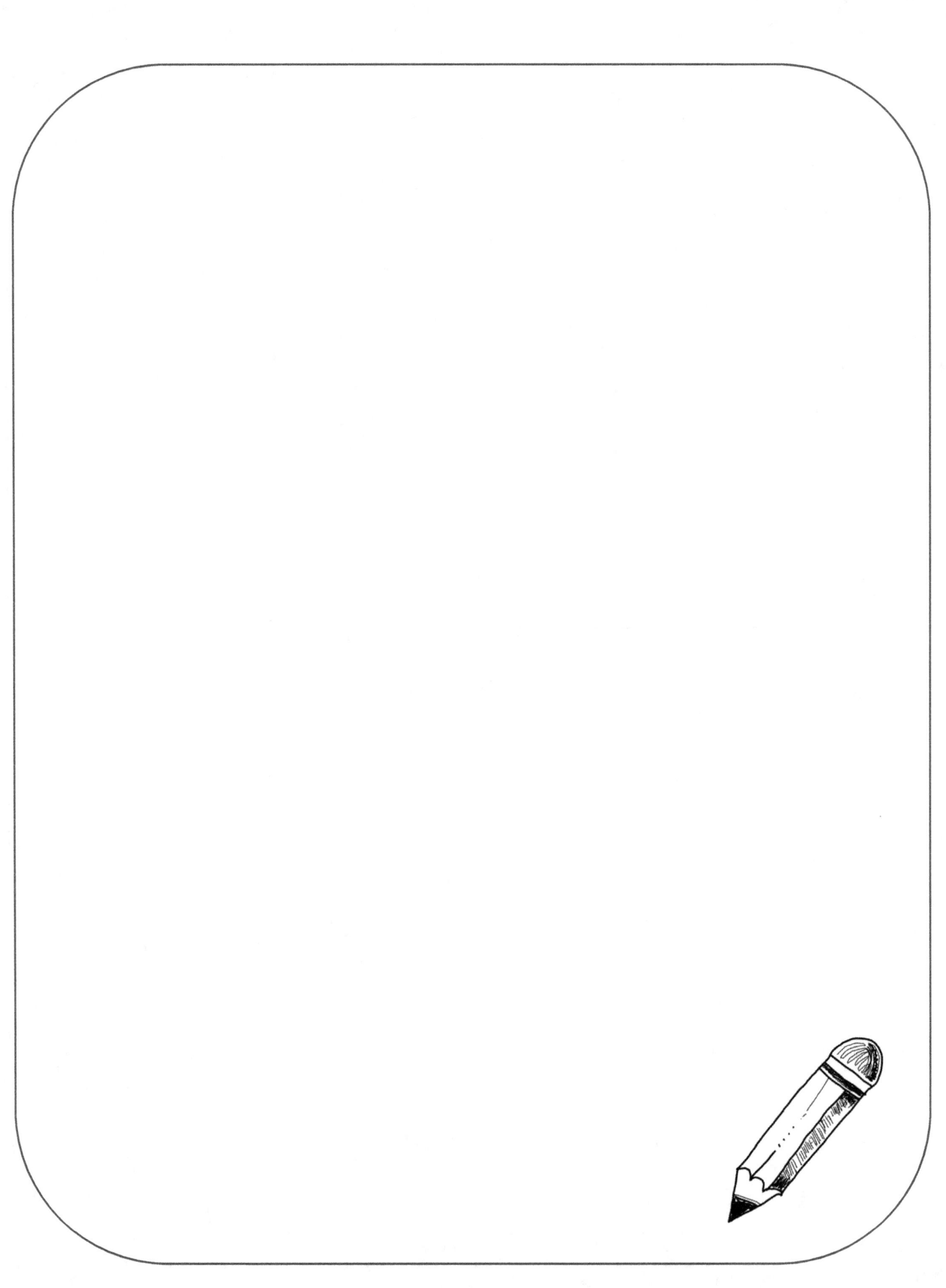

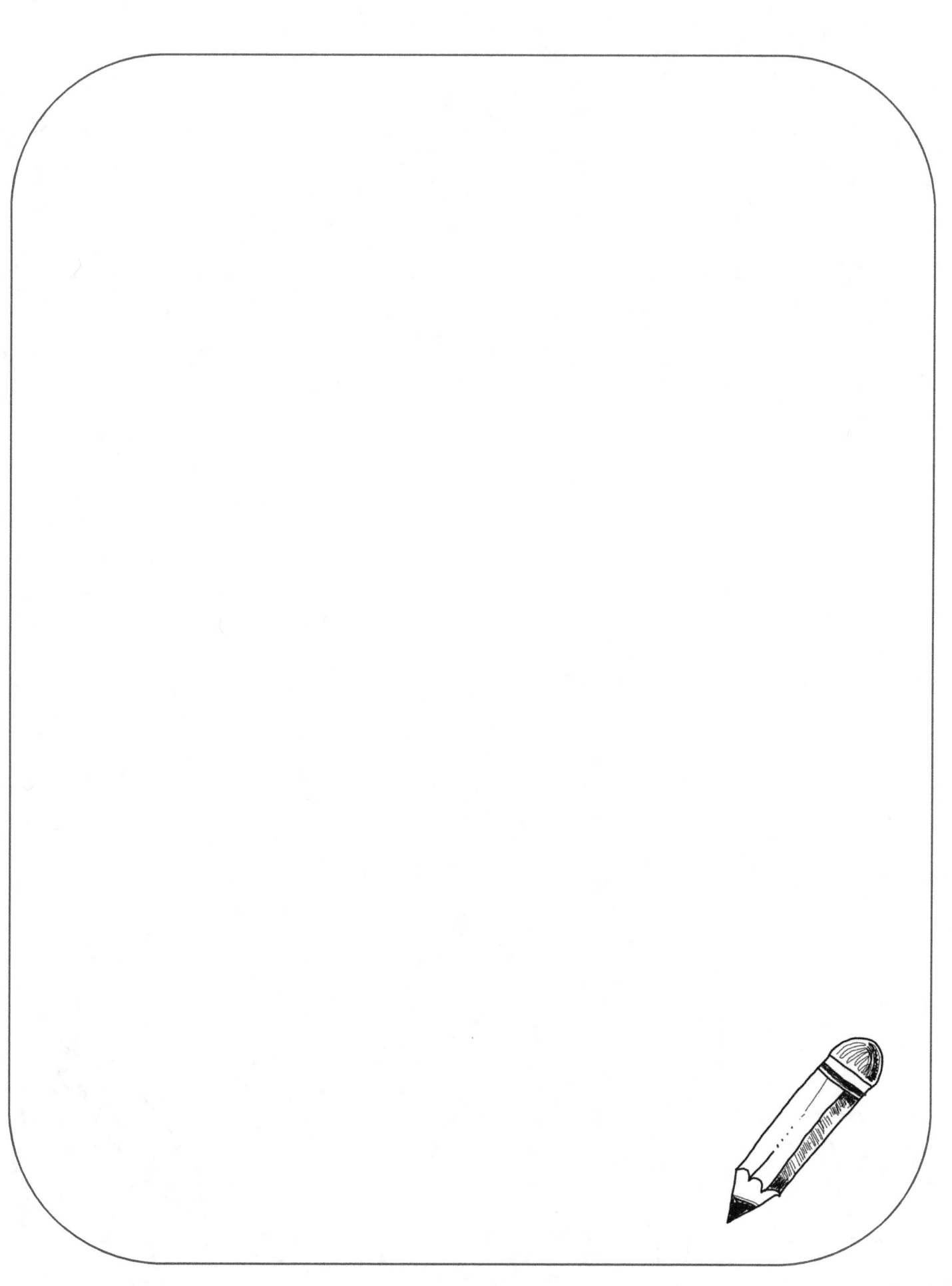

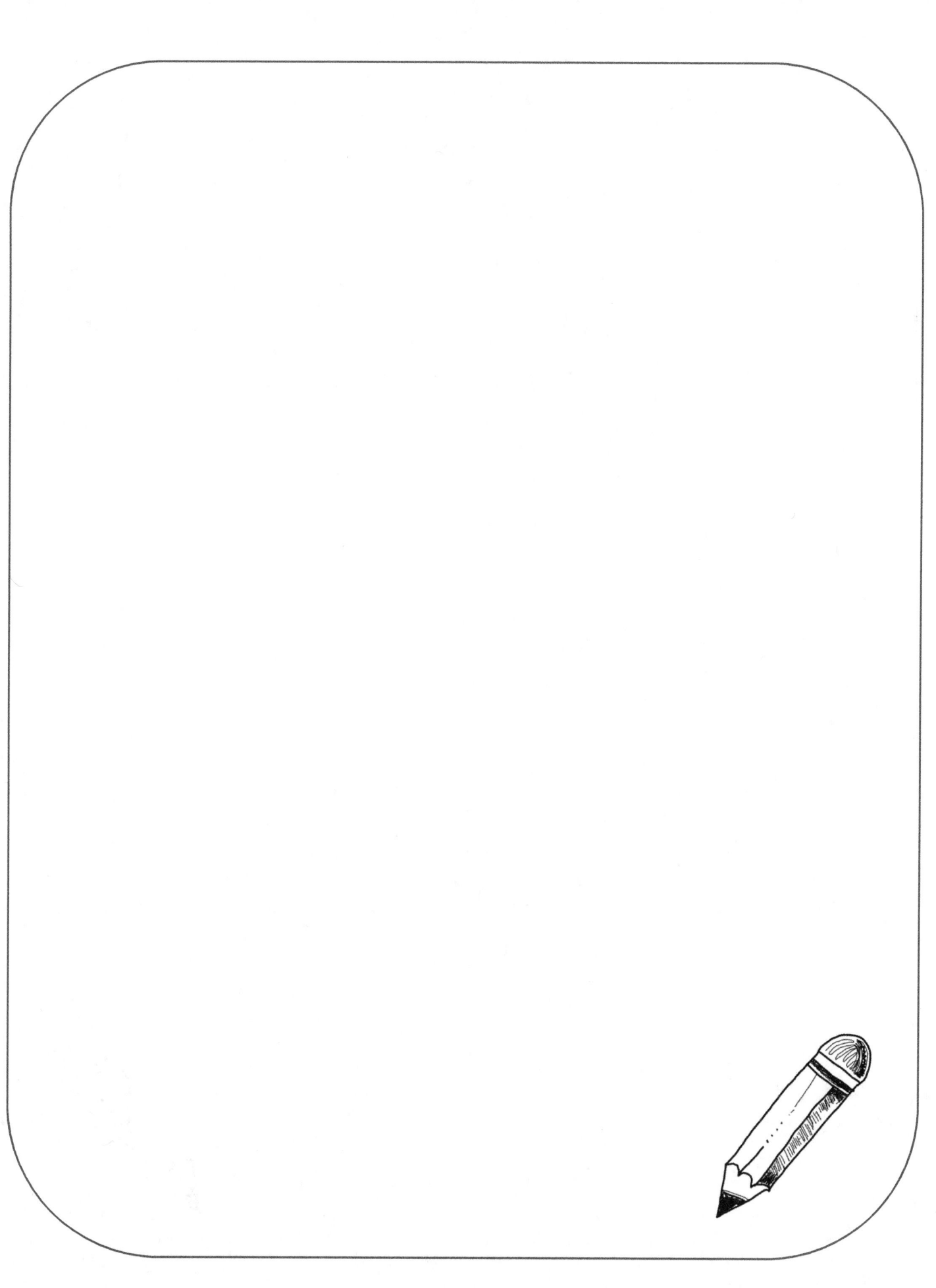

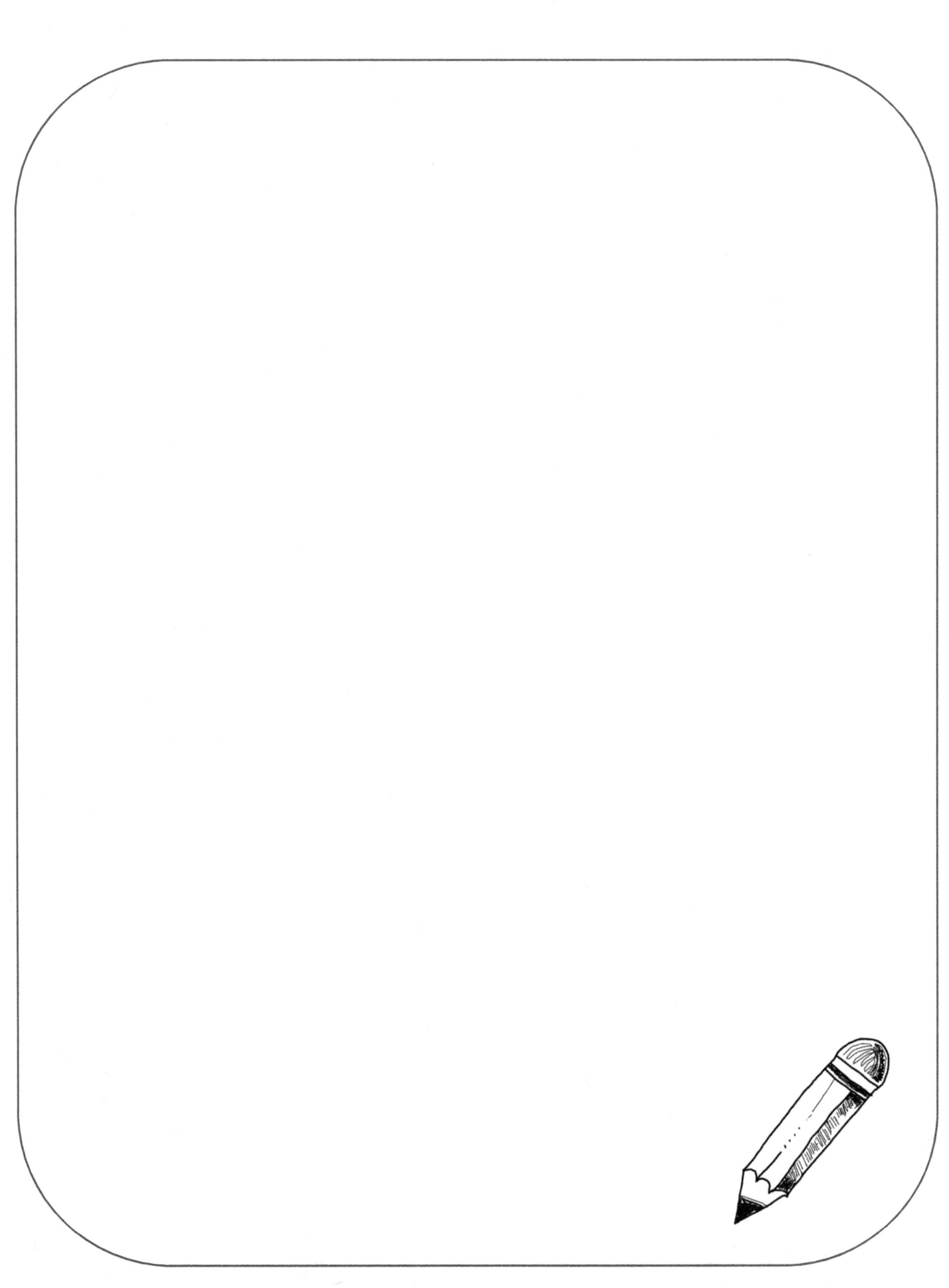

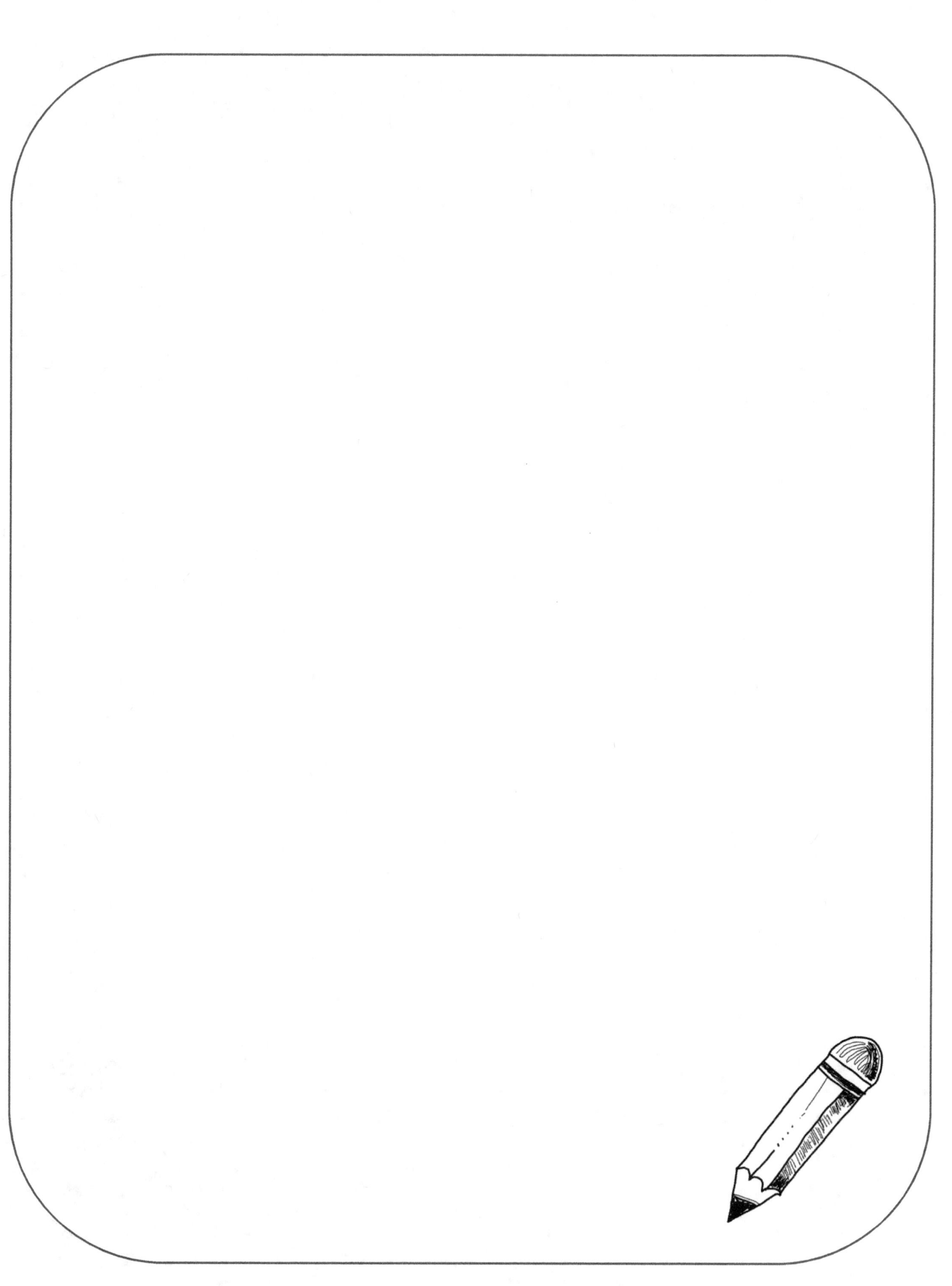

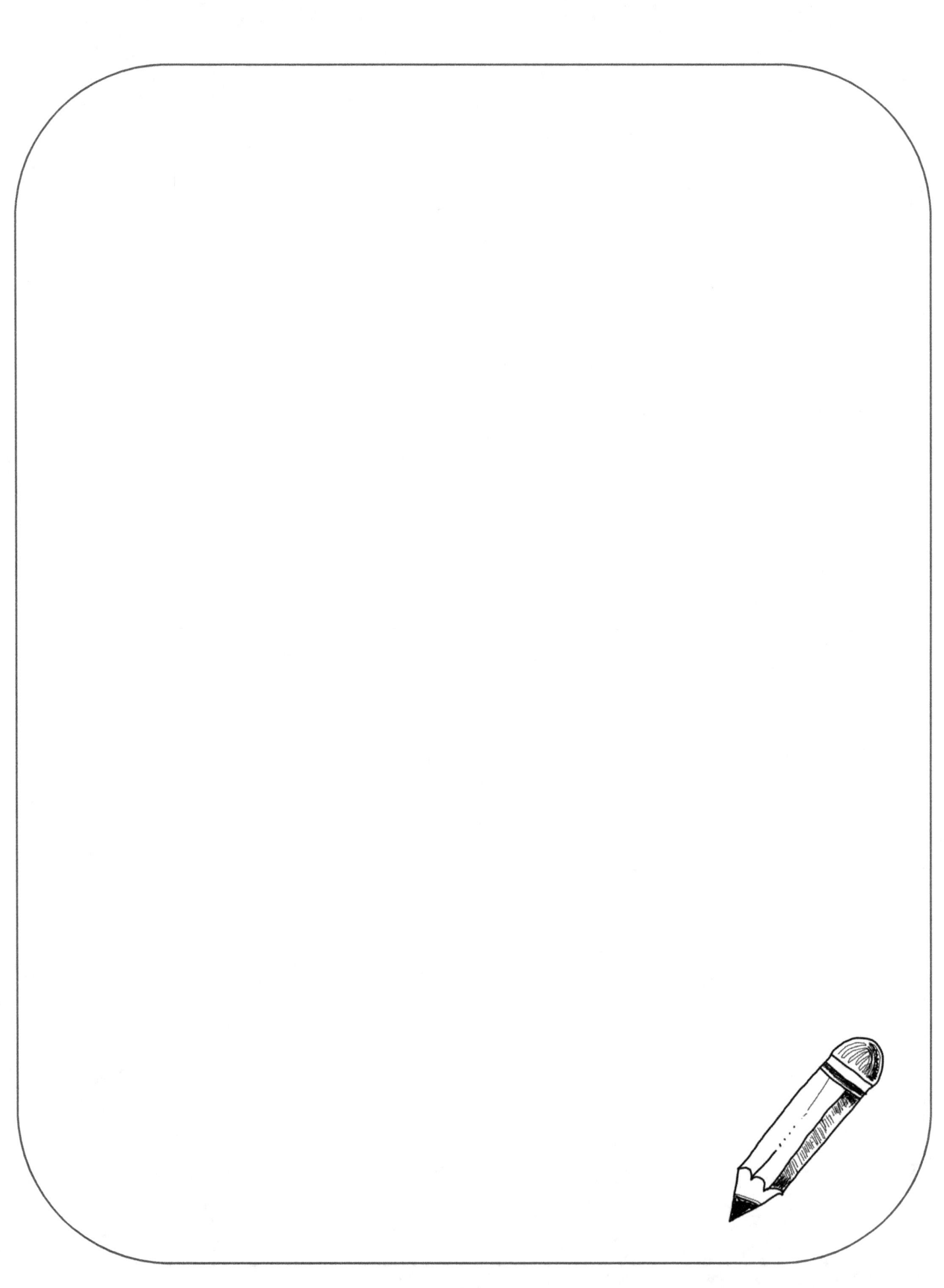

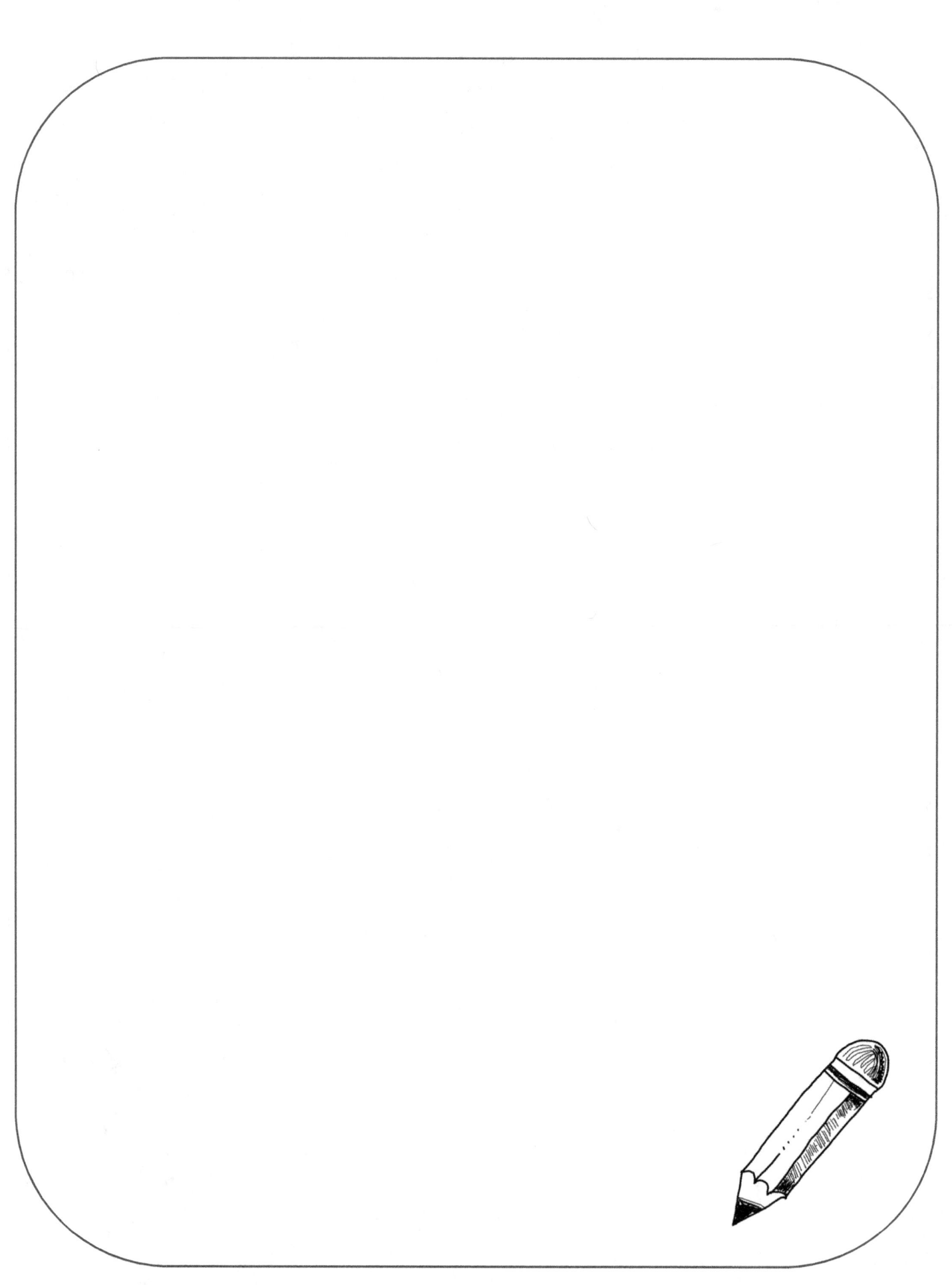

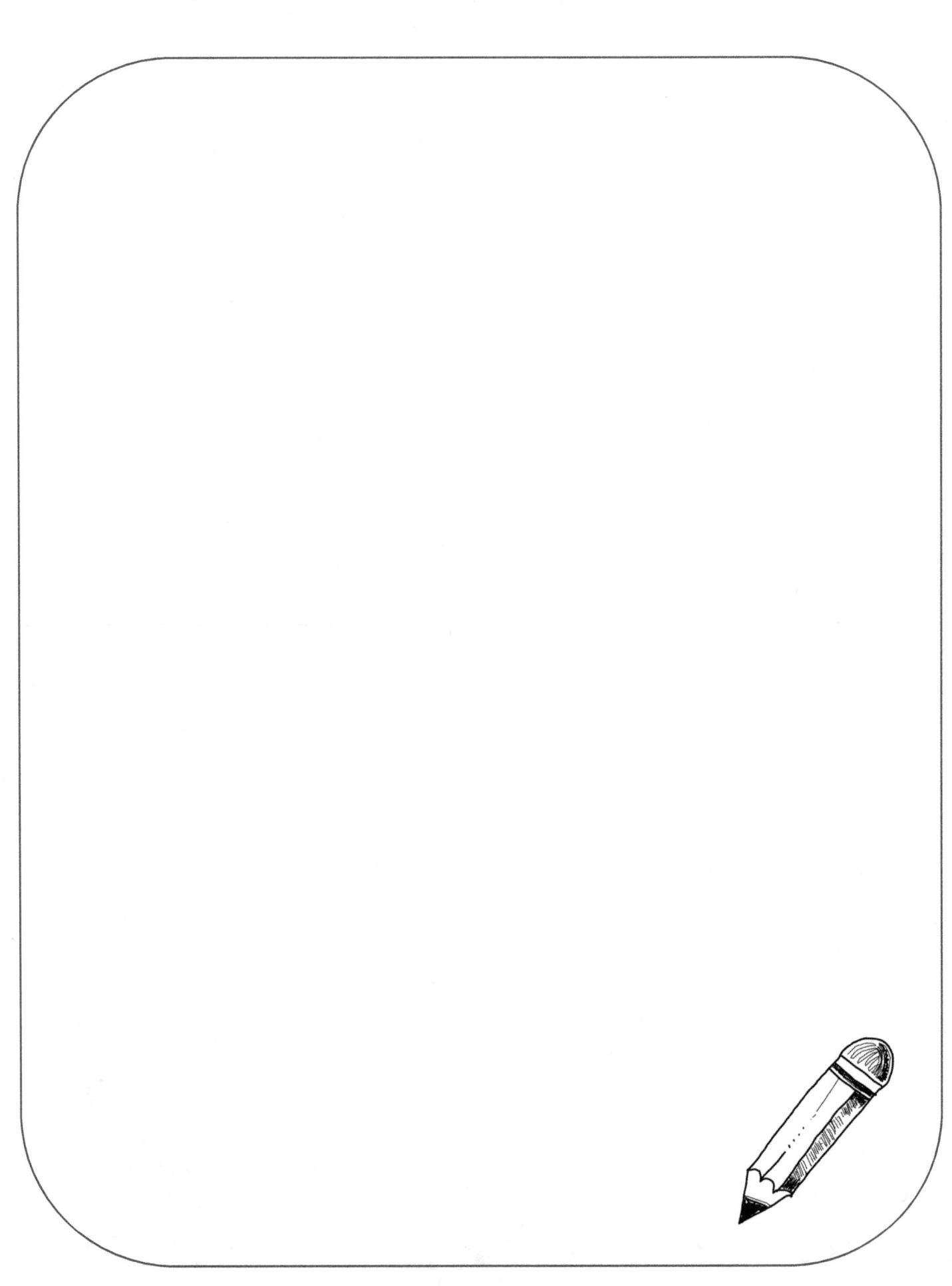

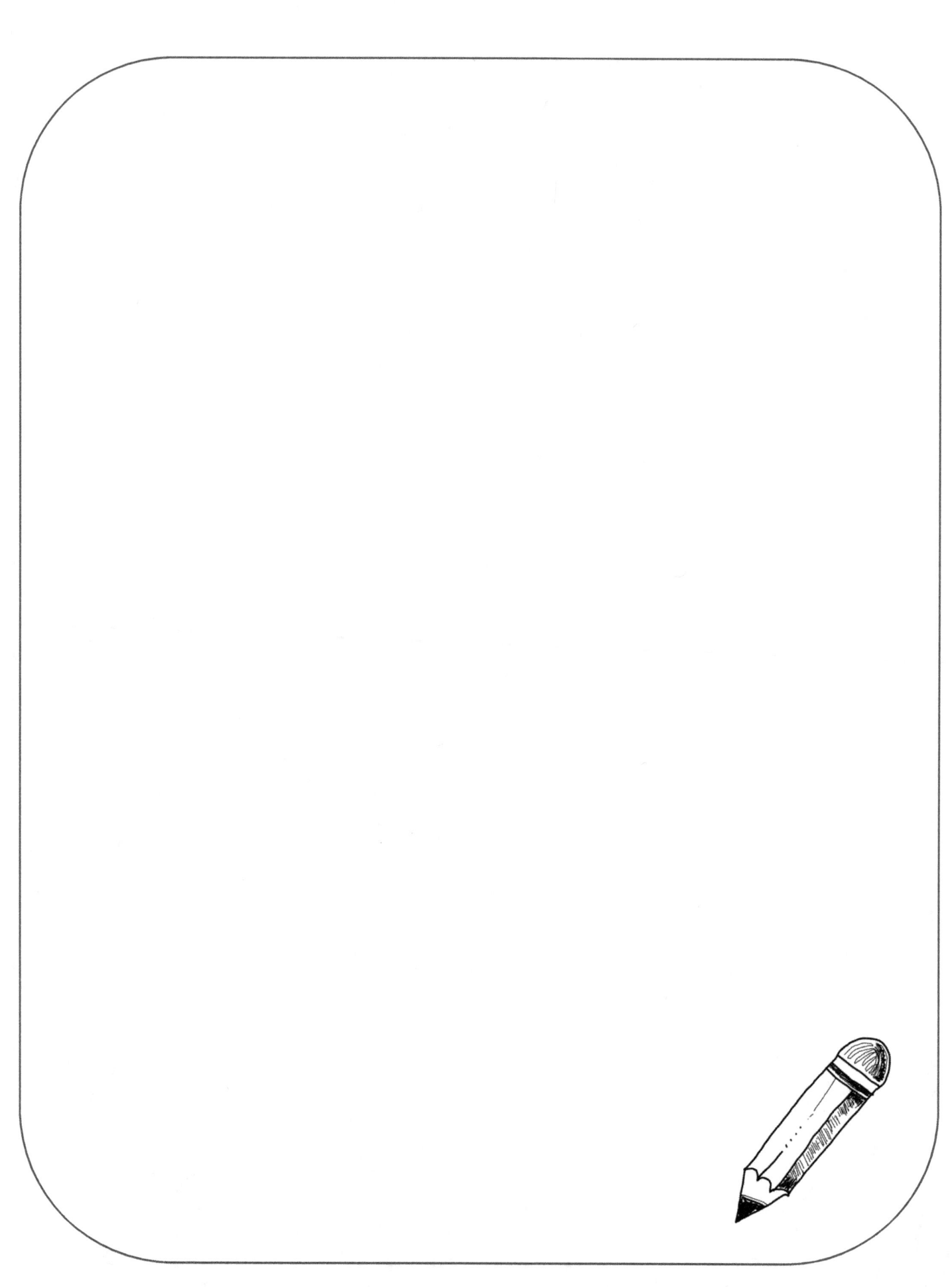

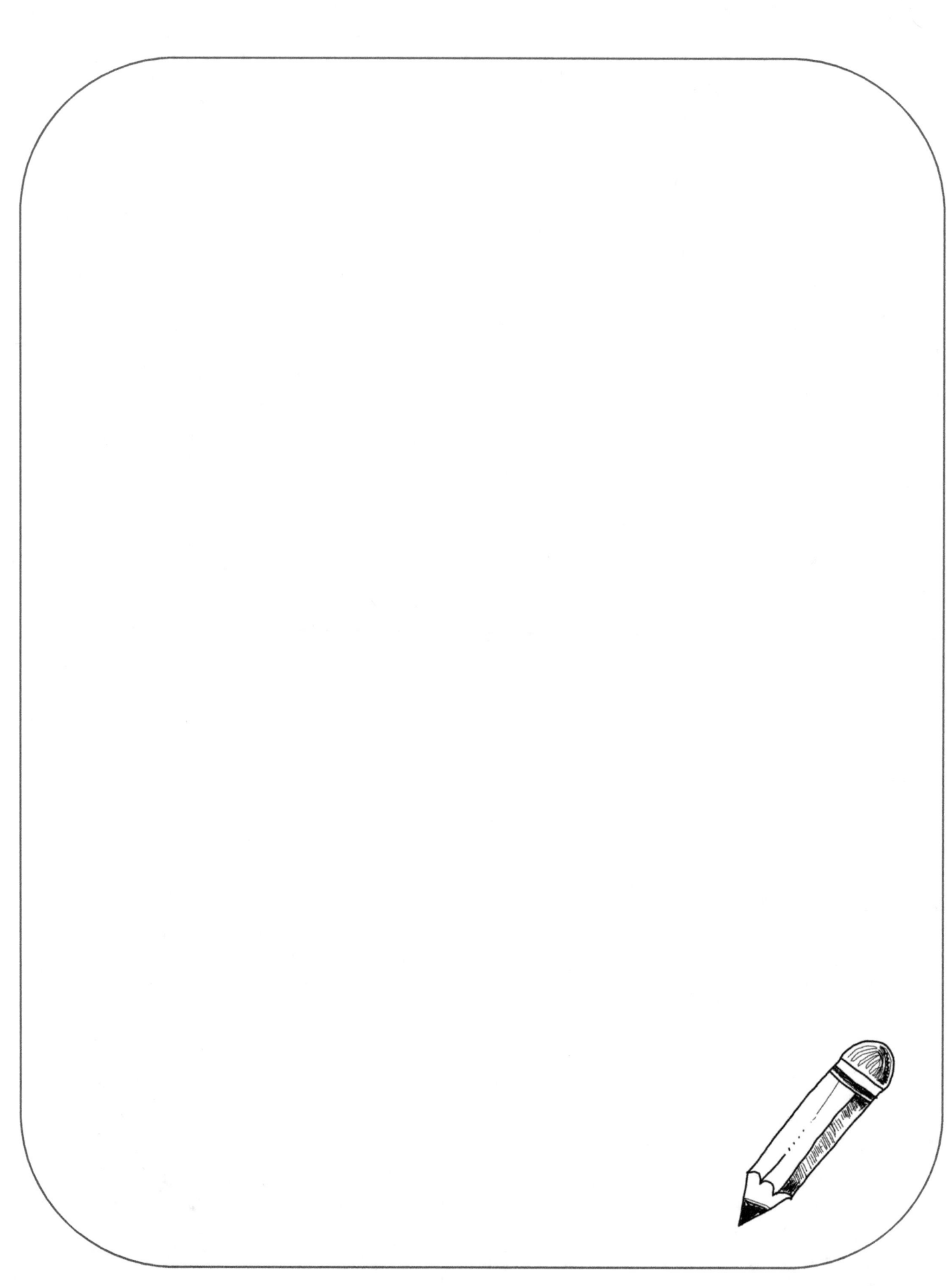

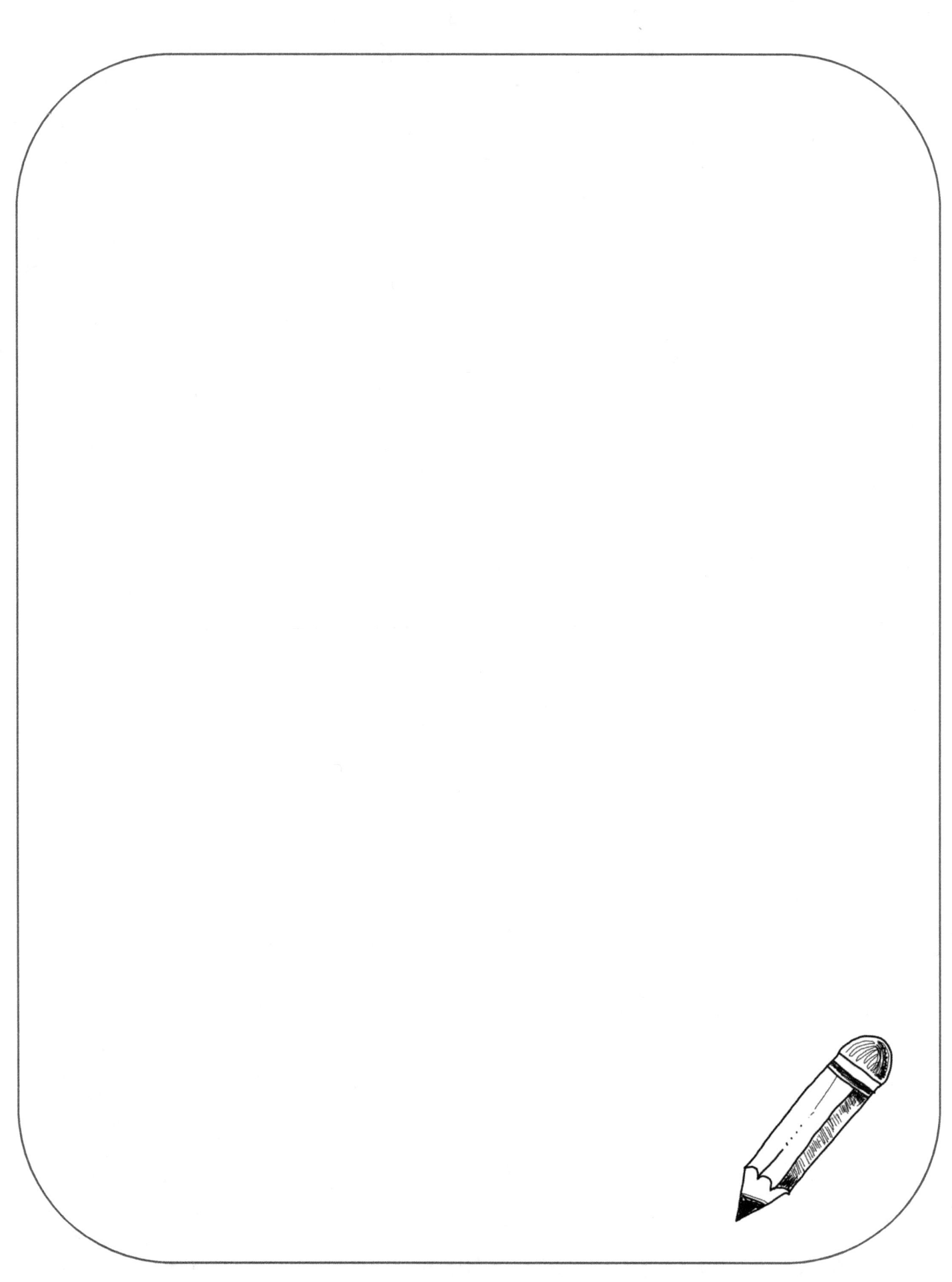

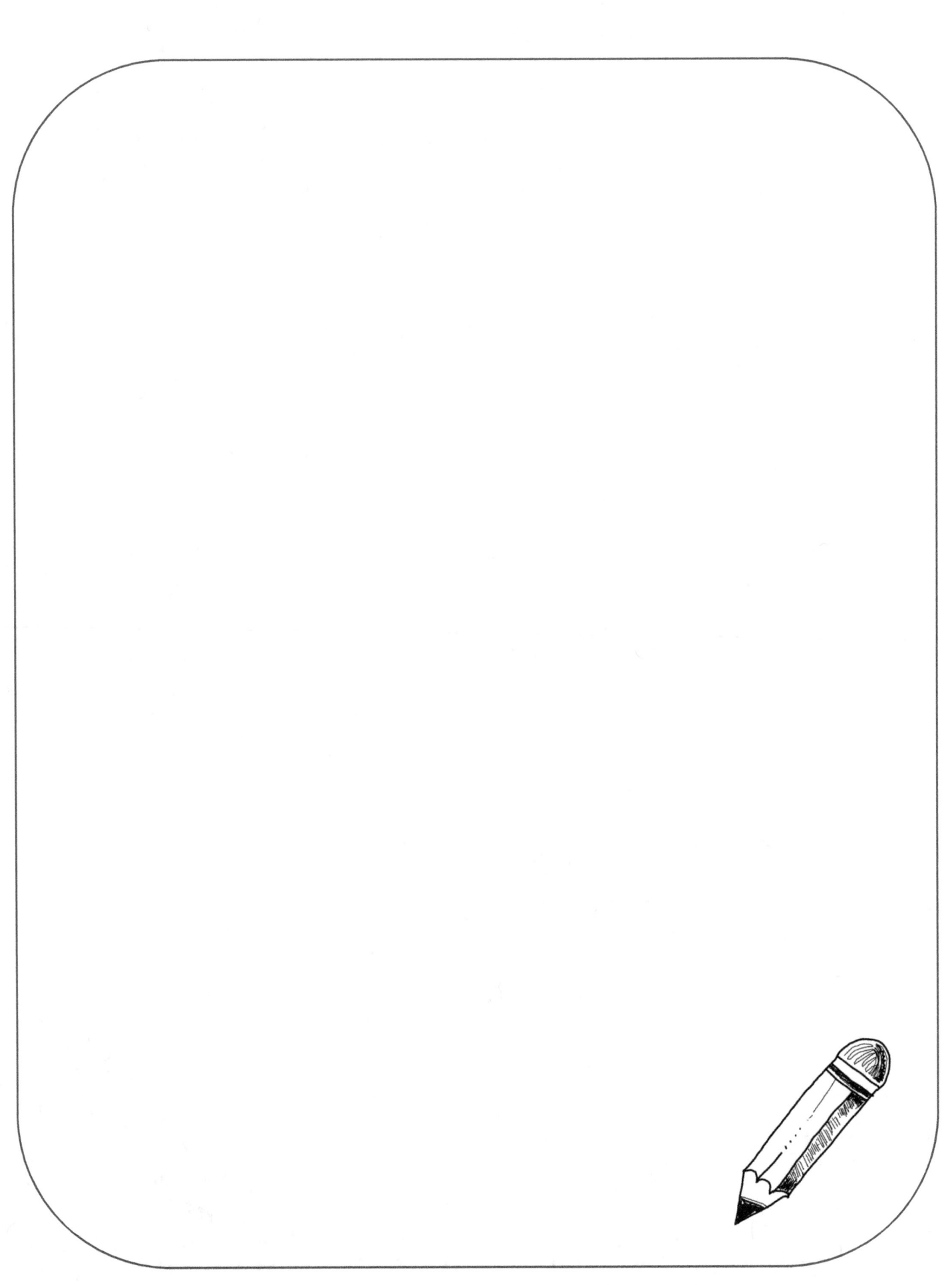

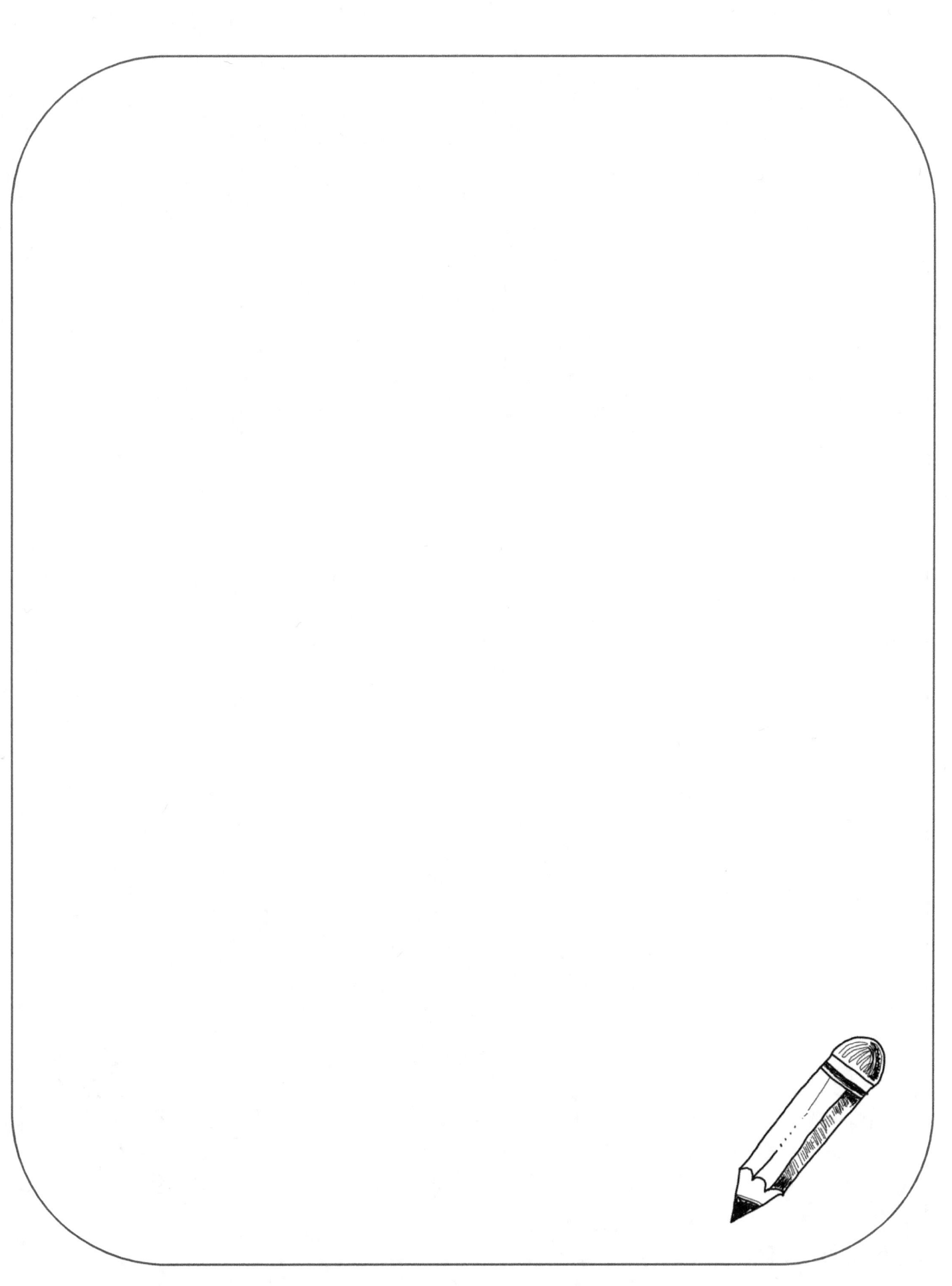

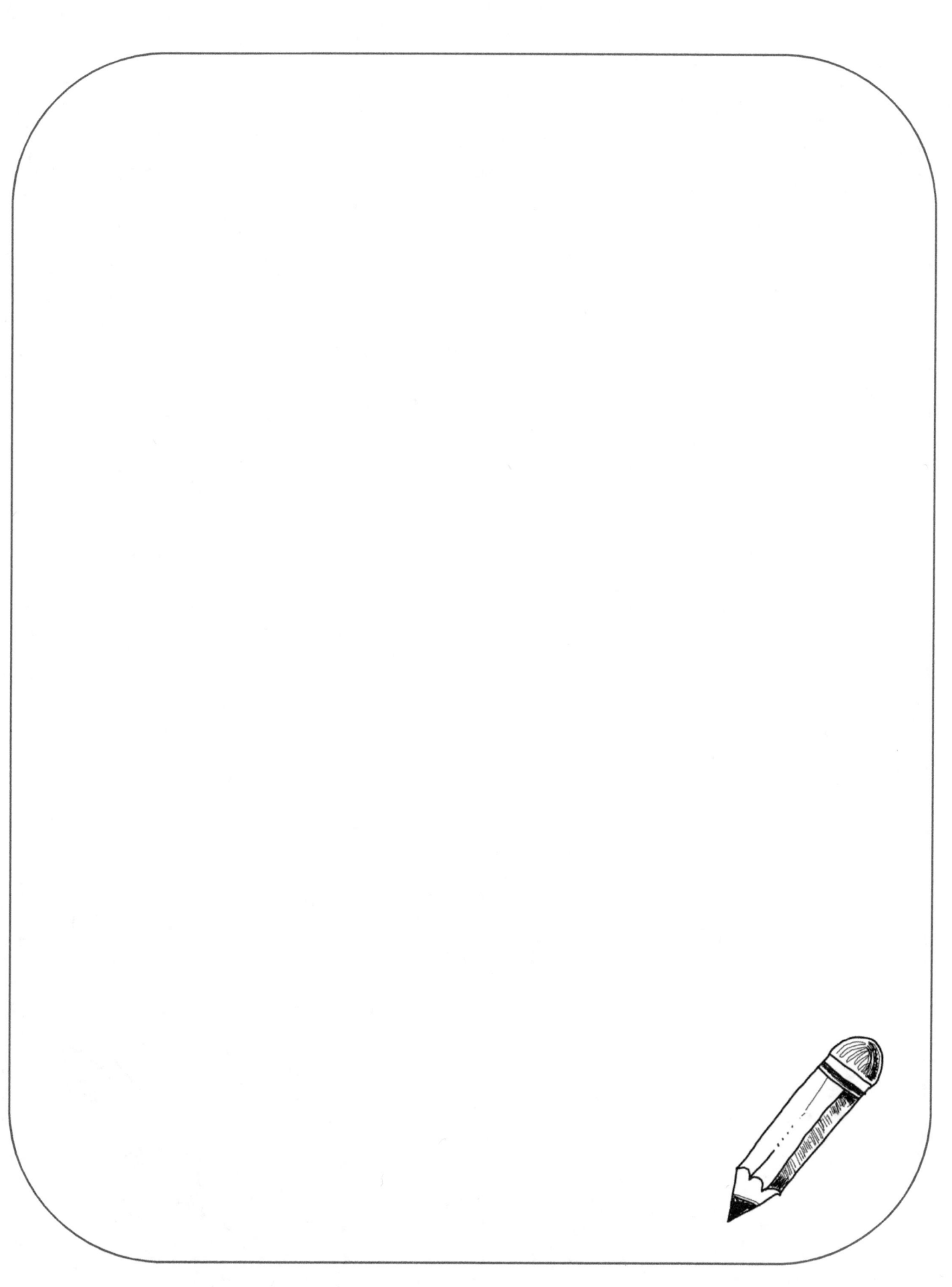

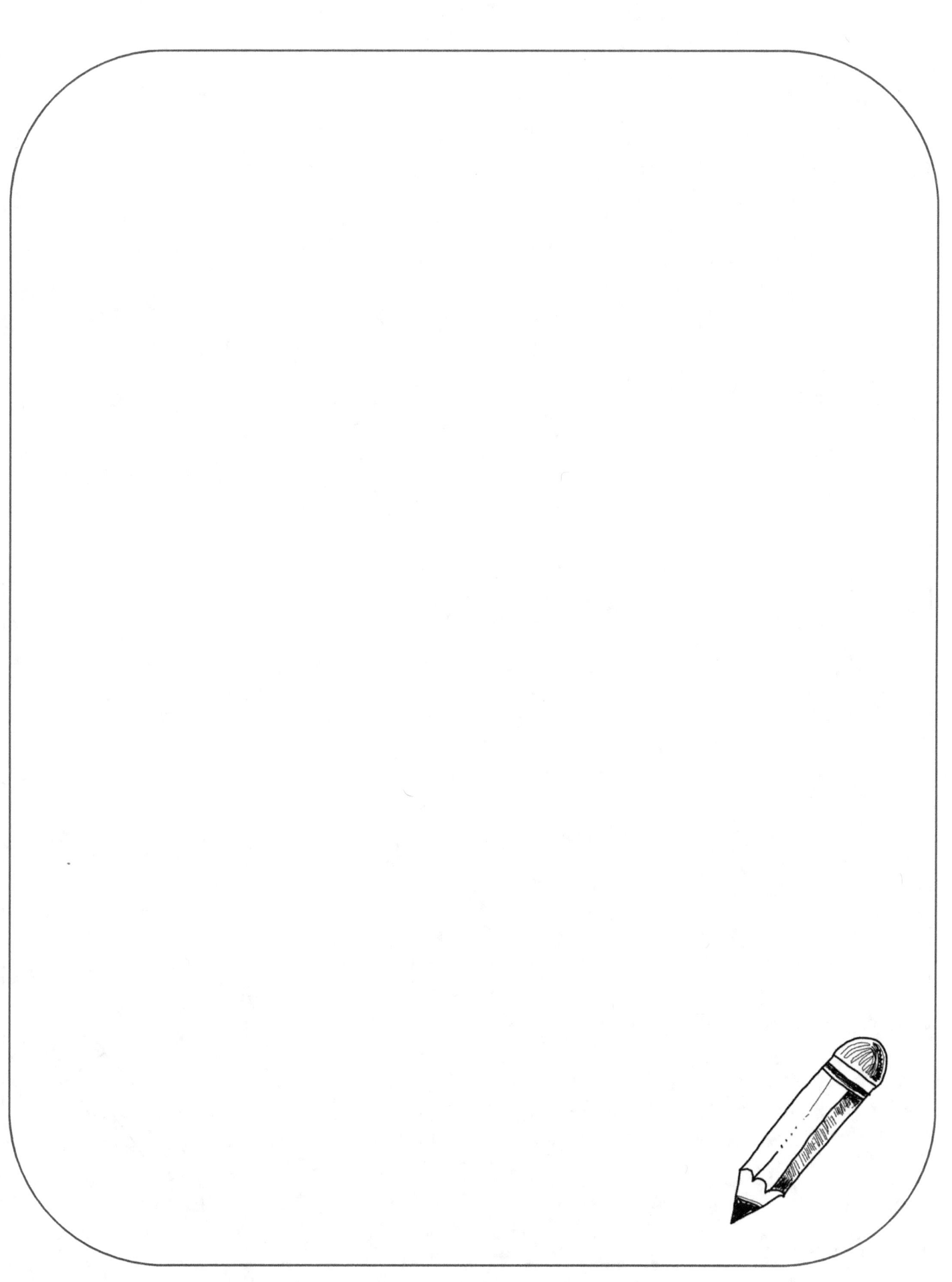

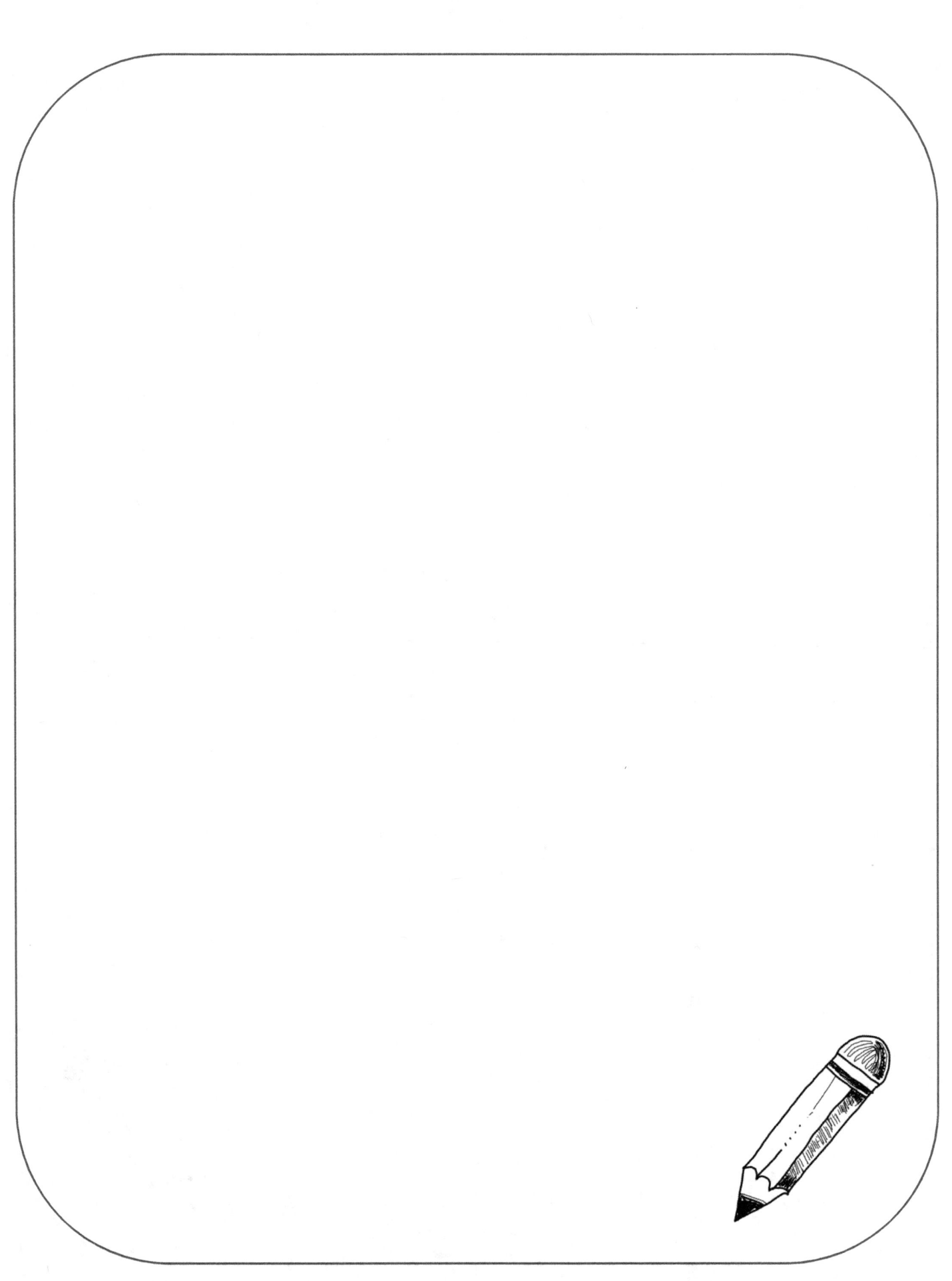

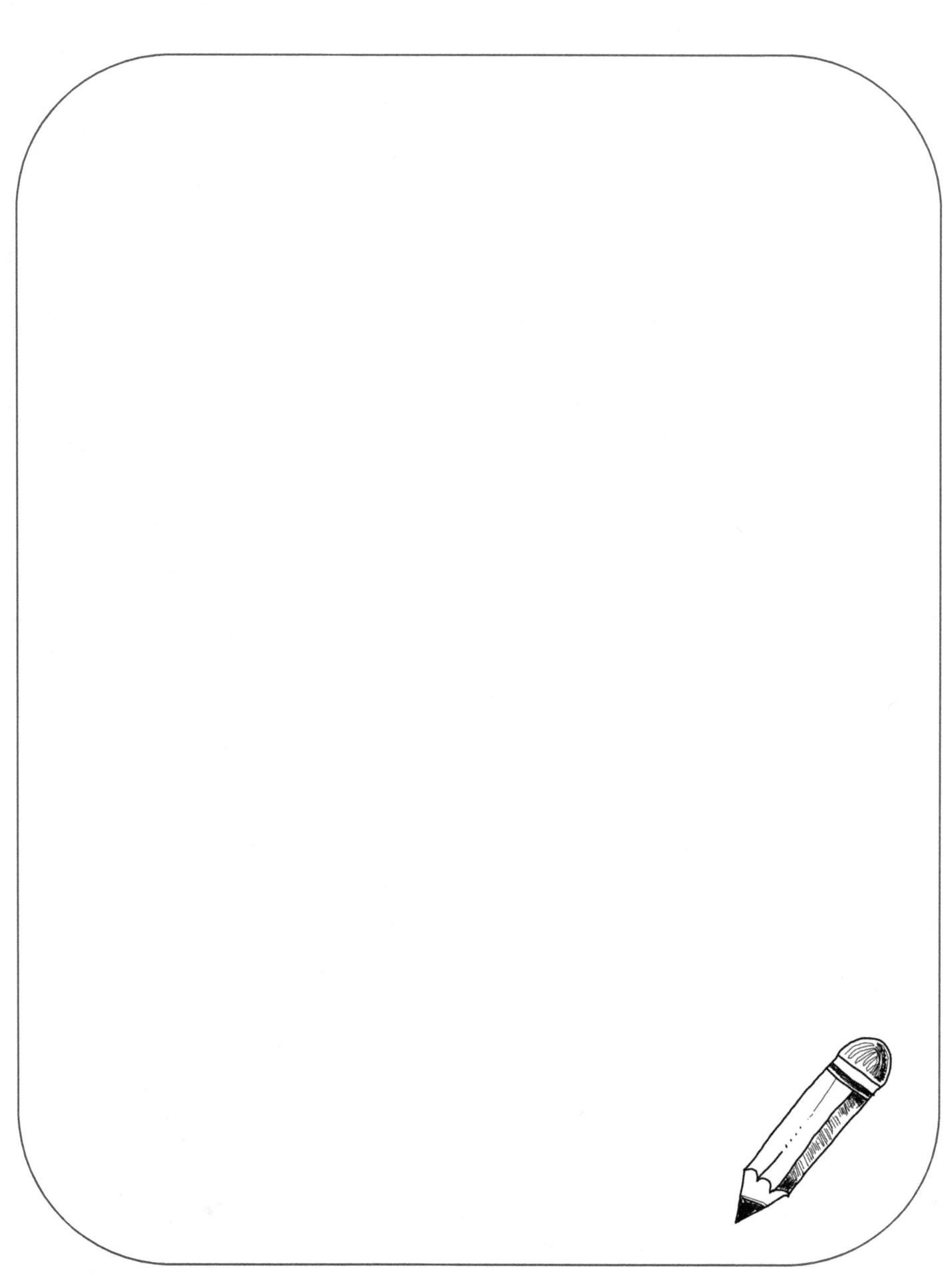

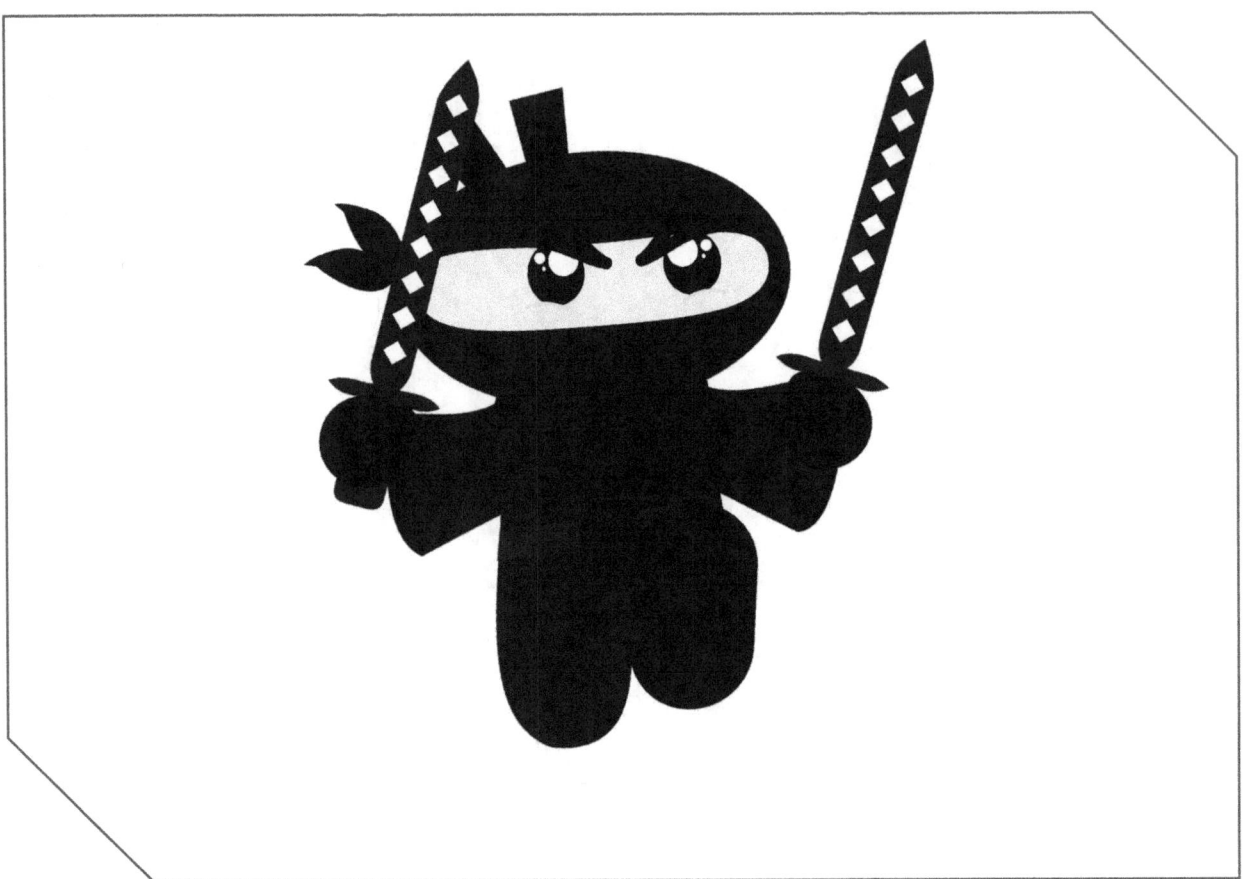

Copyright 2018
Cool Journal Creations

www.ingramcontent.com/pod-product-compliance
Lightning Source LLC
Chambersburg PA
CBHW062330220526
45469CB00008B/2657